Sherlock Holmes Stories

LEVEL 4

Original story by: Arthur Conan Doyle
Re-told by: Andy Hopkins and Jocelyn Potter
Series Editor: Melanie Williams

Pearson Education Limited
Edinburgh Gate, Harlow,
Essex CM20 2JE, England
and Associated Companies throughout the world.

ISBN: 978-1-4479-3129-4

This edition first published by Pearson Education Ltd 2014

11

Text copyright © Pearson Education Ltd 2014

Set in 17/21pt OT Fiendstar
Printed in China
SWTC/11

Illustrations: Paul McCaffrey

Published by Pearson Education Ltd

For a complete list of the titles available in the Pearson English Kids Readers series, please go to
www.pearsonenglishkidsreaders.com. Alternatively, write to your local Pearson Education office or to
Pearson English Readers Marketing Department, Pearson Education, Edinburgh Gate, Harlow, Essex CM20 2JE, England.

The League of Redheads

One day, I found my friend Sherlock Holmes with a large man with red hair.

'Come in, Watson!' Holmes cried. 'Mr Wilson is telling me a strange story.' He turned to the large man. 'Dr Watson helps me with my detective work.'

Wilson showed us an old advertisement. 'It began with this,' he said.

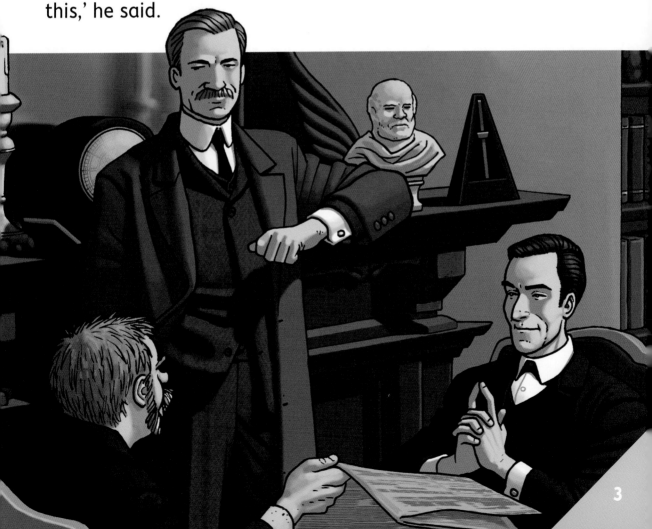

'I have a shop which isn't doing well,' Wilson said. 'My assistant, Vincent Spaulding, works hard for little money. He showed me this advertisement eight weeks ago. Yes, it was strange – but the money was good!'

'On the Monday, we closed the shop and went to Pope's Court. There were hundreds of men with red hair in the street! But Spaulding pushed his way through them. We saw a man called Mr Ross.

Ross pulled my hair and looked at it carefully. "Yes, it *is* your hair. It's a beautiful red," he said. "The job's yours!"'

'I asked Ross, "But what's the job?"

He smiled at me. "It's easy. You sit here for four hours a day and copy a dictionary. You bring the writing paper and we pay you at the end of every week."

Spaulding said quickly, "And I can open the shop."

I took the job. "You can start tomorrow," Ross told me.'

'That night, I couldn't sleep,' Wilson told us. 'Was it all a dream? But it wasn't. Next morning, Ross was in his room with the dictionary. Then he left.

For four hours a day, for eight weeks, I copied that dictionary. Then, one day, I found this card on the outside of the door: *The League of Redheads is closed.*'

Holmes and I laughed.

'That job was important to me,' Wilson said angrily, 'and now I can't find Mr Ross. Was it ... a game?'

'Perhaps,' Holmes said, 'but it was an expensive game. They paid you £32. Tell me ... Your assistant told you about the advertisement. When did he start working in your shop?'

'About a month earlier.'

'Can you describe Spaulding?' Holmes asked.

'About thirty, small, no beard ... a scar on his face.'

Holmes smiled. 'Perhaps I know who he is!' he said quietly. 'Give me two days,' he told Wilson.

'It's a strange story,' I said, after Wilson left.

'It is – and it isn't,' Holmes said. '*Hmm*. Now the League's closed. What's going to happen?'

Holmes looked carefully round the square, then knocked on the door of Wilson's shop. A young man – Spaulding – came out, and Holmes asked him the way to a different street. Then we walked round two corners to a finer street, of shops, restaurants and banks.

'We have to stop a thief – tonight!' Holmes said suddenly. 'Meet me at home later.'

That night, I found two men with Holmes in his flat. We went back to the fine street near Wilson's shop, into a dark building and down into an underground room.

'Watson,' Holmes said quietly, 'Officer Jones hopes to catch John Clay, a thief. Mr Merryweather works for this bank. There's £30,000 here and he doesn't want to lose it.'

We waited. Suddenly, two men climbed up through the floor into the room. Holmes quickly caught the first man. The second man ran outside – into the arms of a policeman.

'Jones,' Holmes said, 'this is Spaulding – or John Clay. You can take him away.'

'Thank you, Holmes,' said Merryweather. 'You saved the bank tonight. You really are a great detective.'

'Clay worked for Wilson,' Holmes told me later, 'because the shop is behind the bank. Because he wanted Wilson away from the shop, he and his friends gave Wilson that strange job. Then he made an underground tunnel – did you see his dirty trousers? – from a room below the shop to the bank.'

'And you caught him, Holmes!' I smiled.

The Three Students

Mr Soames visited us in Holmes's flat.

'I live and work in a college,' he told us. 'Today, I left an important exam paper on my desk and went out. An hour later, I came back and, to my surprise, there was a key in my door. My servant, Bannister, left his key there by mistake.'

'This is my problem, Mr Holmes. The exam paper had three pages. But I found the first page on the floor, the second on a table, and only the third on my desk! Who moved them after I left? I asked Bannister, but he didn't know. He felt terrible about his mistake with the key, and had to sit down.'

'On the table,' Soames said, 'there were small pieces of wood and lead from a pencil. Did a student try to copy the paper? Did he break his pencil and then sharpen it? There were also little balls of clay on my desk.'

'Interesting,' Holmes said. 'Let's go to the college and look at the room.'

Holmes looked carefully round the sitting-room. 'A student took one page at a time to the table by the window and started copying. He broke a *blue* pencil – look! – with soft lead. On your desk, yes, pieces of clay. Which chair did Bannister sit in? This one? And is this your bedroom door?'

We walked into the bedroom.

Holmes opened a cupboard door. 'More clay!' he said.

'After you came back, the student hid here. Then you called Bannister and the student couldn't leave. How many students use the stairs outside your door?'

'Three,' Soames answered. 'Gilchrist is an excellent student who enjoys sport. Ras, an Indian, works hard. McLaren is lazy and has problems with exams.'

Bannister came into the sitting-room. He looked very unhappy.

'After Mr Soames told you about your key,' Holmes said, 'you sat down. But why in *that* chair?'

'I don't know,' Bannister answered.

We visited the students' rooms.

Gilchrist was tall and welcoming. Ras was small and quiet. Holmes asked them for a pencil and looked at the two pencils carefully.

McLaren did not open his door. 'Go away!' he shouted.
'I'm studying for my exam!'

'Is McLaren shorter
than Gilchrist?' Holmes asked.

'Yes,' Soames told us.

'Only a very tall man could see the exam paper from
outside, through your window,' Holmes said. 'Please bring
Bannister and Gilchrist to your sitting-room. Gilchrist
copied the exam paper – and Bannister knows it.'

'You saw the exam paper, Gilchrist,' Holmes said, 'and then Bannister's key in the door. You came in and put your sports shoes on the desk. Clay from the sports ground fell off them. You started copying the paper, then Mr Soames came back. You ran to the bedroom – with your shoes, but without … ?'

'My gloves,' Gilchrist said quietly.

'Bannister saw your gloves on the chair,' Holmes said, 'and sat on them. But why did he help you?'

'I was his father's servant,' Bannister said quietly. 'I love the boy.'

'I'm very sorry,' Gilchrist said sadly. 'Bannister spoke to me earlier. I'm not going to stay at college. I'm going to go and work in Africa.'

'Good!' Holmes said.

Before You Read

❶ There are two stories in this book. Look at the picture on page 3.
1 Answer the questions below. Write a, b or c. What do you think?

_____   _____   _____

a Which man lives in the flat? ☐
b Which man is his friend? ☐
c Which man do they not know? ☐
d Which man has a problem? ☐
e Which man is a famous detective? ☐

2 Read page 3 quickly. Then write the men's
names under the pictures above.

❷ In the second story, there is a
problem with an exam paper.
The exam is the next day.
Talk about this picture. What is
the problem? What do you think?

Activity page ❷

After You Read

❶ **What happened first in the first story? And then?**
Write the numbers 1–6.

a Holmes told the police and a bank worker about a thief. ☐
b Wilson's job finished and he visited Holmes. ☐
c Holmes saw Spaulding, and the bank near Wilson's shop. ☐
d Spaulding showed Wilson an advertisement. ☐
e Holmes and the police caught the thieves. ☐
f Wilson started a new job and Spaulding made a tunnel. ☐

❷ **Write the names from the second story.**

> Holmes   Watson   Soames   Bannister   Gilchrist

a Who left an exam paper on his desk? _____
b Who left a key in the door by mistake? _____
c Who went in and started copying the exam paper? _____
d Who saw some gloves and sat on them? _____
e Who left clay in a bedroom cupboard? _____
f Who looked for a blue pencil in the students' rooms? _____
g Who tells the story of Holmes's detective work? _____

❸ **Talk about these questions.**

a In the first story, why was red hair important?
b Why was a scar important to the story?
c In the second story, why did Holmes look for a tall sportsman?
d How and why did Bannister help the student?